Na Momi Hoʻomanaʻo

Pearls to Remember

Aloha from Hawaiʻi nei!
Barbara S. McDonagh

Written and Illustrated by
Barbara S. McDonagh

Liko PUBLISHING
Kealakekua, Hawaii

ACKNOWLEDGMENTS

Mahalo nui loa to the following: My mother for her support and encouragement; Diane McGregor, project advisor; Charlotte Donat, editorial assistance, Harold H. P. Teves for the cover design.

Na Momi Hoʻomanaʻo
Pearls to Remember
Text Copyright © 1993 by Barbara S. McDonagh
Illustrations Copyright 1993 © by Barbara S. McDonagh
All rights reserved. No part of this book may be reproduced or transmitted in any form or by any means, electronic or mechanical, including photocopying, recording, or by any information storage and retrieval system, without permission in writing from the publisher. Send all inquiries to the publisher.
Published by Liko Publishing, P.O. Box 673, Kealakekua, HI 96750.
First edition 1997

This book may be ordered by mail from the publisher. *But try your bookstore first!*
Library of Congress Catalog Card Number 735-789

McDonagh, Barbara S.
Na Momi Hoʻomanaʻo
Pearls to Remember
Summary: A loved one lost; a friendship cherished; a treasure of experiences shared; a new way of life. How wonderful, the Grace of God!
1. Bereavement; 2. Friendship; 3. Hawaiian culture

ISBN 0-9643781-1-6
Limited First Edition
Printed in Canada

Dedication

To my father, who left me with the message to
be thankful to God for everything.
And to Kekai, who gave me this same message
and who inspired me to pass his knowledge on.
BSMcD

Alphabetical Glossary of Hawaiian Words:

okina – the symbol (ʻ) is used to show a stress syllable, such as ʻupena with the emphasis on the "u."

kahako – the symbol (–) above a vowel that makes the vowel sound long, such as pōhaku.

ʻAʻā (Ah-ah) – rough, jagged lava rock

Ahupuaʻa (Ah-hoo-pooh-ah-ah) – rectangular-shaped land divisions usually extending from the uplands to the sea

Ala hele (Ah-lah hay-lay) – pathway, route

Aloha (Ah-low-ha) – love, mercy, compassion, greeting

Aloha Kakahiaka (Ah-low-ha Kah-kah-hee-ah-kah) – good morning

Aloha nui loa (Ah-low-ha new-ee low-ah) – very much love

ʻEhu kai (Ay-who-kye) – sea spray blown by the wind

ʻEke huluhulu (Eh-kay who-loo-who-loo) – gunny sack; cotton bag

ʻEnenue (Eh-nay-new-ay) – rudder fish

Hale (Hah-lay) – house

Holoholo (Hoe-low-hoe-low) – to go out for pleasure; walk around. (It is a tradition for a Hawaiian fisherman not to confess his intent to go fishing so that the shark will not hear of it and lay in wait for him.)

Hoʻomanaʻo (Hoe-oh-mah-nah-oh) – to remember; to commemorate

Iʻa (Ee-ah) – fish

Kahu (Kah-hoo) – shepherd, minister, reverend, pastor

Kala (Kah-lah) – unicorn fish; several species of surgeonfish

Kanaka (Kah-nah-kah) – mankind

Ke Kahakai (Kay Kah-hah-kye) – the beach; the seashore

Kekai (Kay-kye) – The Sea (proper name in this instance)

Koʻele (Koe-ay-lay) – large opihi

Komo mai (Koe-moe my) – welcome, come here

Lanai (Lah-nye) – porch, veranda

Lei (Lay) – garland, necklace of flowers

Leinaʻala (Lay-nah-ah-lah) – Necklace of Mist (proper name)

Liko (Lee-koh) – New Leaf (proper name)

Limu (Lee-moo) – seaweed; general name for all plants living underwater

Limu Kohu (Lee-moo Koh-hoo) & Limu Kala (Lee-moo Kah-lah) – different types of edible seaweed

Limu Lipoa (Lee-moo lee-poh-ah) – popular, edible type of limu, used as a breath freshener

Lūʻau (lew-ow) – Hawaiian feast

Mahalo nui loa (Mah-hah-loh new-ee loh-ah) – thank you very much

Makai (Mah-kye) – towards the ocean; in the direction of the sea

Makua kāne (Mah-kew-ah kah-nay) – father

Malihini (Mah-lee-hee-nee) – newcomer, stranger

Manaʻo (Mah-nah-oh) – thought, idea, meaning

Manini (Mah-nee-nee) – convict tang fish

Mokunui (Moe-koo-noo-ee) – "Big Island" (nickname of a big rock)

Naʻau (Nah-ow) – bowels, guts; from deep down; of the heart or mind

Na Momi (Nah moe-mee) – pearls

Na poʻe O Nāpoʻopoʻo (Nah poh-ay Oh Nah-poh-oh-poh-oh) – the people of Nāpoʻopoʻo

Opihi (Oh-pee-hee) – limpet that lives on the ocean rocks

Paʻakai (Pah-ah-kye) – ocean salt

Pali (Pah-lee) – cliff

Pāhoehoe (Pah-hoy-hoy) – smooth, unbroken type of lava

Pakuʻikuʻi (Pah-koo-ee-koo-ee) – surgeonfish with striking orange markings at the base of the tail

Papa (Pah-pah) – reef

Pīkake (Pee-kah-kay) – Jasmine; fragrant small white flowers

Plumeria (Plew-mare-ee-yah) – frangipani flower; used for leis

Poʻe O Hawaiʻi (Poh-aye Oh Ha-vye-ee) – the people of Hawaiʻi

Pōhaku (Poh-hah-koo) – rock, stone

Puhi (Poo-hee) – eel

ʻUpena hoʻolei (Oo-pen-ah Hoh-oh-lay) – cast net

ʻUpena kuʻu (Oo-pen-ah koo-oo) – standing net

Wana (Vah-nah) – sea urchin with long, pointed, dangerous spines

To Our Adult Readers...

The Pearl

A pearl is a product of pain. For some unknown reason, the shell of the oyster is pierced and an alien substance, or grain of sand, slips inside. On the entry of that foreign irritant, all the resources within the sensitive oyster rush to that spot and begin to release healing fluids that otherwise would have remained dormant. And, as the irritant sand is continually converged upon by the healing fluids, a pearl is being made. . . .

Nā Momi Hoʻomanaʻo

Pearls to Remember

Chapter I

Na Lei Aloha
Leis of Love

*L*iko silently finished her breakfast, kissed her mother good-bye and set out once again down the mountain to the little fishing village of Nāpoʻopoʻo. She thought of *Kekai,* as she had done so many times since their first meeting.

She had first seen him walking along the beach carrying his *ʻupena hoʻolei* over his shoulder, intently searching the sea for *iʻa* and moving with lightness and grace upon the *papa*. To Liko, Kekai was massive. It was not just his six-foot frame, nor his 275 pounds that struck her so, but the impact of his presence. It was as if he was a magnet drawing her to him. Thus, she found herself following behind him despite the fact he was a total stranger.

The sea, the sunshine, the moment seemed to breathe more deeply around him. His enjoyment of life was so great that he could not contain his own excitement! It bubbled out of him and filled Liko's heart with a smile. And it was still so with Kekai. Never had she met another person who took such a joy from life itself!

Today was the start of another beautiful morning on Kealakekua Bay. Liko was no longer a *malihini* here. *Na poʻe o Nāpoʻopoʻo* knew her by the name Kekai had given her and would smile and call out, *"Aloha Kakahiaka,* Liko," as she walked along the path to Kekai's *hale*.

Today was the start of another beautiful morning on Kealakekua Bay.

Usually Liko skipped and ran in short, joyful spurts toward the haven of Kekai's friendship. But today her world was full of sadness. Her head was down. She did not see the warm gestures of the village people.

When she reached Kekai, she called, "Kekai, Kekai."

Kekai answered, "Aloha, Liko! *Komo mai.*" As always his *aloha nui loa* was real and true and any other time it would have flown on the wings of his smile right into her heart.

Liko looked up. "My father has died," is all she said to him.

For a moment they just stood there looking out at the sparkling sea and tears began to stream down their cheeks. Kekai was crying with her. Then he said gently, "He was very sick and we've been expecting this, Liko. He's with the Lord now. Everything is going to be alright."

Through her grief this thought reached her because she believed in Kekai.

"Go and make some *leis* and we will have a simple ceremony here, on the water, for your *makua kāne.*"

Liko went to the local church yard and picked many *plumeria* flowers and strung them into four leis. For so long her father had been away from her, living on the mainland. This last year of his life had been spent in the hospital. She had felt so helpless and useless to him. Now, she was doing something meaningful just for him. This soothed the pain and consoled her.

For a moment they just stood there, looking out at the sparkling sea.

On the way back to Kekai's she found some bushes of *pīkake* in full bloom. She picked them also and carefully strung these fragrant, tiny white flowers into a fifth beautiful lei. This must be what heaven smells like, she thought.

She returned to Kekai's hale with her five leis on her arm. Kekai took them from her and carried them, resting lightly on his hand, his arm held up high, as together they swam out to *"Mokunui."*

Mokunui was Liko's rock. A short distance from the shoreline, Mokunui was named "Big Island" because it was always above water, even at the highest tides. Liko often swam to this rock. It had a natural seat and a niche where she could find shelter from the wind. From this perch Liko would drink in the beauty of the sea. The past months she had looked out across the bay and thought of her father.

Now Kekai and Liko sat upon Mokunui and Kekai said a prayer that was filled with comfort and hope. She cried as he spoke. Then he cast a lei onto the water. Liko cast her leis one by one as she sobbed and said a final "aloha" to her father.

For a while they watched the leis carried to and fro by the waves. Then Kekai broke the silence. "We have emptied ourselves of sadness. Now let's go and eat a nice cold slice of watermelon so we can fill ourselves up with joy."

Liko did not want to leave the rock and the leis and swim away. But Kekai was quite insistent. By the time Liko reached the shore she felt much better.

Kekai knew this when he asked her, "Do you want a big or little slice?"

She answered, "A **very** big slice!"

They laughed for the first time that morning and stood leaning over Kekai's *lanai*, eating watermelon, spitting the seeds out, and watching the leis floating about the rock.

Now Kekai and Liko sat upon "Mokunui" and Kekai said a prayer that was filled with comfort and hope.

Later that evening, as the sun was starting to set, Kekai saw four of Liko's leis still floating around Mokunui, and the fifth lei floating in the distance.

Liko went to the water the next morning, looking for the leis to be washed up on the shore somewhere. She walked quite a ways along the shoreline, but she never saw them again.

Later that evening, as the sun was starting to set, Kekai saw four of Liko's leis still floating around Mokunui, and the fifth lei floating in the distance.

Chapter II

Ke Kahakai
The Beach

As time went by, Kekai watched Liko growing up. She was taller now. Her legs were getting longer and she could keep up with him as he walked on the ʻaʻā. He included her in many experiences. How she loved to watch Kekai as he readied himself to throw his net upon the water! He took on an intensity that glowed with excitement – the fisherman tapping into the treasures of the sea. He awaited his moment, and then he threw.

As Kekai's net came up filled with fish, it would thrill her and she would exclaim, "OH!" in a high pitched shriek. This always made him look back at her on the beach, putting his fingers to his lips and beaming with pleasure. Then he would shake his head, reminding her to be quiet. Her happiness magnified his own. They were a team!

Many times Kekai had told her that when throwing net he did not just see the fish but knew where they would most likely be, in the channels and holes of the reef. "By the action of the waves, I know how the fish will react. As the wave comes in, the fish turn toward the wave. As the wave goes out, they turn back in toward the shore. The very moment when they are turning, that is what I wait for! Then I throw my net."

Ke Kahakai – The Beach

She tried to help as much as she could. The older she became, the more responsibilities he gave her. She was his "bag girl" on these excursions. When Kekai threw his net and caught fish she would carry them in a bag that was tied around her waist. It was called an *'eke huluhulu*. He had shown her how to fashion it and she had sewn it up herself.

She kept a knife in the bag just as Kekai had taught her, so she was ready to gather *opihi* should she come upon it while going *holoholo*. She also carried Kekai's opihi knife, which they laughingly referred to as "The Persuader" because it was so big.

On her first trip with him, Kekai taught her about opihi. "Opihi is a half-shelled creature that likes the *makai* side of the rocks and takes its nourishment from the sea. The rougher the waves, the more the opihi like it."[1]

Kekai continued, "The opihi usually picks big rocks that do not move to hang on to. If it is on a small rock, it has to be wedged in between large rocks so its foundation will be solid. People should be more like opihi – safe and secured on the rocks, never giving into the waves, as people are safe and secure in God's love and care, never giving into the ways of the world."

He also told her, "If you're angry with someone, never go holoholo. You should always have a good feeling when you go.

"Never eat food while harvesting it at the sea. The *po'e o Hawai'i* believe the waves will become angry and make it dangerous to gather more food. It does not matter whether it is opihi, *limu, wana* or *i'a*. No eating until you are out of the water! You must be very respectful as you are taking the sea's bounty from her."

… so she was ready to gather opihi … she also carried Kekai's knife, which they laughingly referred to as "The Persuader" because it was so big.

He explained to her, "It is also an important job to watch the fisherman and be there in case help is needed."

He taught her to never walk ahead of him when he was throwing his net because he was capable of seeing fish way ahead in the water. He would always be cautious and quiet in his approach. Also, if he needed to throw his net quickly, she would be out of his way. She also learned to stop when he stopped and walk when he walked.

One day he suggested, "Let's go holoholo and see if the big fish have come in." It was always an adventure to accompany Kekai. This was Liko's favorite pastime. The day would unfold in ways that were not predictable. The ocean spoke to him of so many things. As they walked Kekai would tell Liko stories only he could read from the lava rocks and the waves.

"See the smooth stones placed among this 'a'ā?" asked Kekai now, as they walked along. He pointed to the *pōhaku*. "This is an old *ala hele* that the people used long ago. They brought the smooth pōhaku here and placed it among the 'a'ā so it would be easier for them to walk. Remember, they walked barefoot. They set the white coral along both sides of the trail as markers so that in the moonlight the coral would reflect the light and help them stay on the trail."

Now that he had pointed it out she saw the large white coral markers and the smooth lava rock in the midst of the 'a'ā.

Kekai continued, "In some places, the men brought the smooth pōhaku eighty feet up the *pali* from the beach. They would place the smooth stones in lengths of an average step. Sometimes the stones are set quite a distance apart and you can tell that the people used the trail for running. This fisherman's ala hele circles our entire island and usually runs parallel to the King's Trail, which is further inland.

"See the smooth stones and coral placed among this 'a'ā?" asked Kekai now, as they walked along.

"There were also the trails of the *ahupuaʻa*. These were rectangular-shaped land divisions usually extending from the uplands to the sea. Many people lived on this land, and they shared their food and natural resources with each other. The wood to make canoes came from the mountains, while the salt and dried fish came from people who lived here along the sea."

Another day as they walked they came upon round holes that were dug out on the reefs for the purpose of making *paʻakai*. Kekai brought her attention to them. "See how the lava has been pounded down to create circular or egg-shaped pools so they will hold sea water? They could be filled in by man or the big waves and high tides would fill them. The sun evaporates the water and leaves a residue of salt crusted on top of it. The fine salt is made from the *ʻehu kai,* the spray that is thrown up into the air by the force of the waves and blown by the wind. When heavy rains come the paʻakai ponds are ruined because they become diluted by the fresh water. See how some of the salt places are natural occurrences among the rocks? This is how the *kanaka* learned to make their own paʻakai ponds."[2]

Liko bent to look more closely. "Oh yes, I see it now!"

Kekai showed her how to collect the salt by skimming up the crust ever so carefully with her hand and pushing it to one side of the pond. "This way, the excess water will drip down. On our way back we can put it in your ʻeke huluhulu and later, at home, you can lay it out on paper in the sunshine and the salt will dry perfectly.

"Look around! See how many pools there are? It took a lot of pools to make sufficient salt for all the people. Salt was used as the main means to preserve food. When I was a child, this is how we always made our salt. We did not go to the store to buy it."

Liko bent to look more closely at the pa'akai ponds.
"Oh, yes, I see it now!"

Liko never tired of these times. The hours she spent with Kekai were like a string of precious pearls. They glowed from inside, and when she was lonely, she sat and remembered each pearl, one by one, and relived each precious moment.

It was at these times that they shared their secrets. Liko's secrets were mostly from her *naʻau*. Kekai's secrets were the salt and the Hawaiian trails, the fish and the waves.

Liko felt Kekai had lots to say and she was more than willing to listen to it all! Whatever struck him as being important for her to learn became another pearl on her string. To Liko, Kekai was important. He was like a treasure chest full of pearls!

"I'm happy I can tell you these things, Liko." Kekai was smiling gently. Then he grew very solemn and said, "Most young people of today find themselves engrossed with the western ways of living and seeking pleasure. They have abandoned all interest in learning about the richness and values of their own culture. I hope you will always remember what I have taught you and use it to your advantage. *Hoʻomanaʻo.*"

"Oh, I will, Kekai. I promise!"

Liko took delight in harvesting salt whenever she found it. She always carried two bags, one for iʻa and one for paʻakai. And she looked for and walked on the ala hele.

On this day they found two kinds of limu, limu kohu and limu lipoa.

One day they set out for fish. The day brought them *limu* instead. Liko had tasted fresh limu before and it was delicious. The iʻa loved it also.

The strong flavor and aroma of *limu lipoa* would often be in the fish that Kekai caught. Liko knew limu was healthy and tasted the best with raw fish. On this day they found two kinds of limu, *limu kohu* and limu lipoa. Both are prized by the kanaka.

The sea was very rough and Liko could not do much gathering. Kekai told her, "Watch the waves so I can concentrate on picking the limu."

When she saw a very big, powerful wave coming, she signaled and shouted to him, and he would back up off the papa to higher ground.

They filled two five-gallon buckets with limu. For days afterwards, Kekai and his wife, *Leinaʻala,* worked long hours cleaning and separating the limu. Every little pebble and grain of sand had to be removed.[3]

Kekai told her, "Watch the waves so I can concentrate on picking the limu."

Chapter III

Na Momi Hoʻomanaʻo
Pearls to Remember

As Liko grew up Kekai saw that she was becoming a strong swimmer, and he sometimes allowed her to help him set the *ʻupena kuʻu*. These are long standing nets, averaging seven feet in height, with floats on top and lead weights holding them down to the bottom.

Kekai set them at night and picked them up the next morning. It was hard work and Liko helped by guiding the net out into the water on an old inflated tube tied to a body board. Another one of her jobs was to carry out the spear when they went to pick up the net. Kekai might have to fight off a *puhi* that was eating at the fish in the ʻupena kuʻu.

Kekai told her, "Now that you are older, Liko, I can depend on you more. Just being in the water with me, and watching so I will not get tangled in the net as I set it, is a big help."

One evening when the bay was very calm, they set two ʻupena kuʻu. The next morning, right after sunrise, Liko and Kekai met to pick up the nets.

"I was up all night worrying about my nets," Kekai told her. "I heard the wind pick up and start really blowing."

And he was right. Liko could see the water had changed. What was usually a calm bay was now a choppy, churning, threatening sea of water.

"Be very careful and stay right with me," Kekai commanded.

One evening when the bay was very calm, they set two ʻupena kuʻu.

As he pulled up the ʻupena kuʻu, Liko held onto the tube and helped by following closely behind Kekai. When the net started to slip off the tube, back into the water, she would, inch by inch, pull it up again. They had caught some *ʻenenue* and *manini,* a large *kala,* and some lobster.

The nets were fine. But Kekai was worried. He had felt a strong crosscurrent as they swam out to the nets. Now, as he made his way back in toward the shore, pulling the body board and about fifty pounds of ʻupena kuʻu and fish on top of it, he looked back at Liko. She was caught in the current and could not make headway.

"Need some help?" he shouted above the angry sea, as he turned to start back for her.

"No, I'm fine!" Liko yelled back.

Kekai continued in toward the beach. After a few seconds he turned again. Liko was still no closer and struggling hard against the currents. Carrying the spear was hindering her further.

He started back for her and she yelled, "I'm fine! I don't need any help!"

No sooner were the words out of her mouth than Kekai was in front of her. "Hold out the spear," he commanded. Through the swirling current, he pulled her safely into the little bay. Without a word, he swam back to get his nets that had drifted out a little and then he swam on to the beach. He did not look back.

Liko had barely reached the shore when Kekai turned toward her, his eyes burning. His voice was low and she could feel his anger was barely contained. "Don't ever refuse help when it is offered to you in the water!"

Liko whispered, "I'm sorry." She was afraid to look at Kekai. She worked, head down, silently beside him. She helped him remove the fish from the nets and refold them as he had taught her.

Liko was caught in the current and could not make headway.

It felt like a long time taking care of both nets in silence. Then Kekai went to clean the fish. Usually, Liko would have helped him. He had taught her how to clean the fish thoroughly, and it was a chore she really enjoyed. But at this moment, he did not want her company.

She stood by the water's edge watching Kekai's back as he cleaned the fish. She felt like the lost and lonely little girl she had been years before when she had first been befriended by Kekai. Looking at the waves she tried very hard not to cry; this pearl was cutting into her heart.

After a while Kekai came over to her and quietly said, "I'm telling you this because I love you. First of all, we're not in our own element out there in the ocean and the faster we get out of the water the less we have to worry about.

"Secondly, the tide was against you and you knew it. By refusing help it only prolonged your struggle and even jeopardized me as I was trying to help you.

"We must always be watching out for one another. By refusing help it sends a message out that says you don't need to be watched by anyone and, in turn, you don't need to watch others."

Kekai asked, "Do you understand?"

She looked up at him. **This** was the pearl that was building within her! It no longer hurt! The beauty of its luster shone through her eyes now. He could see pools of understanding. If she spoke, she would cry aloud, so she nodded "yes" instead.

"I'm going holoholo. Would you like to come along?"

"Oh! Yes!" she exclaimed.

He was smiling now.

They had caught some 'enenue and manini, a large kala, and some lobster.

She grabbed her bag and headed off behind Kekai. She kept just far enough behind him that her shadow and her movement would not cause added alarm to any fish within his net's reach.

After some throws and some success, Liko and Kekai stood together looking out at the sea. Kekai spoke. "I always try to find a friend to go holoholo with because it is not safe to go alone. Danger can strike fast, without warning, and the helping hand of another can determine whether it will be a disaster or just a minor mishap.

"One day I went holoholo with a friend. He was picking limu kohu at the edge of the papa. The waves came up and over gently onto the reef and then moved slowly out and over the sea back into the ocean. The depth at this particular place was close to sixty feet.

"Without warning, a wave came back onto the papa, sweeping my friend gently into the water. He knew how to swim and although he had the look of surprise and concern on his face, he kept trying to find a place to come back up on the reef.

"I had seen this happen before and I knew just how he felt. Even though he was a good swimmer, I jumped in also to give him assurance and be by his side. It was a while before the waves subsided and we could find an easy exit from the ocean, but we made it back safely together.

She grabbed her bag and headed off behind Kekai, keeping just far enough behind him that her shadow and her movement would not cause added alarm to any fish within his net's reach.

"Sometimes we are best of friends with someone until the water gets a little too deep, and we back off. My friend had needed help, any kind of help – a rope, a life-saving ring, a tube, something. All I had to give was myself. I did not touch him. I was just there, swimming along with him. He thanked me when we got to shore and our friendship grew stronger."

"I felt so ashamed," Liko explained. "There you were, loaded down with all the nets and I could not take care of myself. I didn't want you to have to help me."

"Never be ashamed to accept help when you need it, Liko! Hoʻomanaʻo."

Liko nodded. She would remember.

Kekai smiled and held up the *pakuʻikuʻi* they had caught on his last throw. They were together as a team once more. He reminded Liko, "These are some of the many experiences and knowledge of the culture that need to be shared with others, and there is so much more for you to learn."

Liko asked, "Do girls cast ʻupena hoʻolei like men do?"

"Sometimes," Kekai answered. "They must be very strong and sure-footed on the rocks. It's more common for the men in the family to catch fish in this way, but women can do something just as important. They can learn to repair the nets and even make them."

"Will you show **me** how?" Liko asked excitedly. She had watched Kekai repairing his nets and always wished that she knew how to help him.

"I will! And I'm sure you will learn to do a good job, judging by the curiosity and persistence that you have." Kekai was smiling broadly. "Come. I will show you how today."

They headed back to Kekai's hale.

They were together as a team once more.

That night, Liko excitedly told her mother about her day's adventures. "And Kekai has started to teach me how to sew a net!" she said so proudly and with such seriousness that it made her mother smile.

Later that evening, Liko knelt beside her bed. She spoke to God. "Thank you, dear Lord, for this day, for all it has given me, and for Kekai." She understood that it had taken Kekai his whole life to learn all that he was teaching her, and he would not be with her forever.

But she had her string of pearls. She would remember them over and over, moment by moment, every precious one. She snuggled warm and safe in her bed as she drifted off to sleep.

The Pearl

Yes, the pearl is the product of a wound that has been healed. As we accept the challenges in our own lives, we will also be building a string of precious pearls.

1. Note about Opihi

When the tide goes down the opihi will move down to be near the water, and in doing so, will leave a round black mark on the rock where it has been. The fisherman, knowing that the tide is dropping, will look close by the mark towards the water and will find opihi there. If it is high tide and the fisherman sees this mark, he knows that someone else has gone ahead of him and has already picked opihi. Avoid picking opihi on rocks that are near or on sandy beaches. The opihi has a tendency to retain sand in it, especially fine sand. Liko knew opihi is a great delicacy to the Hawaiians, and no *lū'au* is complete without it.

There are three common types of opihi: the ones that live on the edge of the reef that are hard and yellow; the dark, soft opihi that live higher and further back from the crashing waves; and, lastly, the ones that live underwater, which are big (3-1/2 inches in diameter). We call these opihi *ko'ele*. They need to be cut up before they are eaten.

2. Note about Pā'akai

The Hawaiians living in the highlands used calabashes to carry salt water home. (Calabashes are dried, hollowed-out gourds used for storing water or food.) The salt water was poured into rocks that had been pummeled out specifically for this purpose. These "salt holes" were covered with big leaves when it rained. In this way salt was readily available for those living far from the sea.

3. Note about Limu Kohu

Limu kohu has to be soaked in fresh water for at least two days before eating. Limu kala is added to help hasten the removal of the bitter aftertaste that is in the limu.

Liko's Photo Album

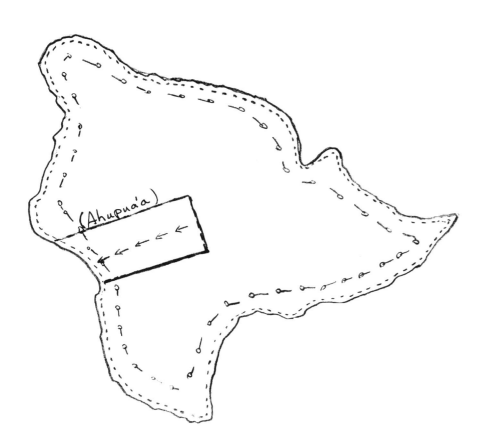

Legend of Trails
Fishermen's Trail ....
King's Trail —o—o—o
Ahupua'a Trail →→→

Ahupua'a Trail from the mountain to the sea

Top Left: The King's Trail

Top Right: The King's Trail 30 miles down the road

Bottom: Kekai is making a new throw net.

Top Left & Right: An Old Fisherman's Trail

Bottom: Kekai is stalking the fish.

Above: Kekai sees the fish.   *Above: He closes in on his target.*

Left: Kekai throws his net...

Right: ...and he catches!

Top Left: My favorite rock, Mokunui

Top Right: Kekai has hung his nets to dry.

Bottom Left: Ah, Dinner!

Bottom Right: Kekai picks the limu while I watch the waves.

Message from the Publisher

This book is a series of stories chronicling the true adventures of two friends, "Liko" (Ms. McDonagh), and "Kekai" *(Kahu* Harold H.P. Teves). It depicts a treasured friendship, and one so rare these days, of mentor and student. Every line was written with mutual consultation and agreement. *NA MOMI HO'OMANA'O* is inherently co-authored, but Kahu Teves insists on stepping back and pushing his protégé forward.

The vision for this project was Kahu Teves' entirely. He chose the stories to be included and set their tone. "Liko's Photo Album" was his idea and the cover is his design.

Ms. McDonagh was blessed to receive the knowledge and insights from her friend by living through the experiences recounted here. Inspired by the great desire of her mentor to share his knowledge, and guided by his deft counsel as editor-in-chief, the accomplishment of this project is more than Ms. McDonagh ever dreamed possible.

It is the hope of these two friends that the old Hawaiian ways will not be forgotten. More important is the intrinsic worth of true friendship: May it warm and encourage yearning hearts and help to illuminate the pearls in each of our lives so that we may discern them, gather them up and hold them fast.

This work is the second installment in a trilogy, the first being MAKANA ALOHA - Gift of Love, and the third soon-to-be-published work, KA 'UPENA - The Net.